Written Words
Never Spoken

Written Words Never Spoken

Ryan Ng

Original cover design by Samantha Araujo
© 2017 Ryan Ng
All rights reserved.

ISBN: 0692907971
ISBN 13: 9780692907979
Library of Congress Control Number: 2017910327
WWNS Publishing, Barnegat, NJ

For everyone I've ever loved and for every love I've ever lost.

Contents

Introduction ix

The Reader and the Writer 1
The Drinker and the Drunk 15
The Sea and the Shore 23
The Dark and the Light 33
The Knight and the Thief 41
The Seasons and the World 51
The Stars and the Longing 63
The Lover and the Dreamer 79
The Lost and the Found 87

Introduction

This collection of poetry started as a personal way to materialize my thoughts. It was simply used as a substitute to say what I wanted to say without the words ever leaving my mouth. The following poems were not originally written for anyone to really read, aside from a few close friends and friends no longer, some of whom may know the stories behind the rhyme. There is no real intended audience, but if there were, it would be anyone who has lived, loved, and lost. The poems mainly focus on the rise and fall of relationships—the beginning, middle, and what comes after. People who were once our everyday company sometimes become strangers who once knew all our secrets. Even if just one poem in this entire collection is relatable to you in some way and helps you breathe easy knowing that you are not alone, then it was all worth it. Some of the content may relate to darker themes or times of internal struggle, but please know that no one is truly alone, even if there are times it may feel like it. Find what brings you peace in moments of chaos, and never let go.

The Reader and the Writer

The Reader and the Writer

I tried to find your love between the lines,
Looking for excuses to keep thinking about you.
You wrote a book I should have hated,
But I read it over and over
Until my hands bled from turning pages
And my pen scribbled all the words I couldn't say.

The sorrow soaks into the page,
Handwritten or by other means.
If I don't write it all down,
It finds its way through my mouth,
Built up behind my teeth—
An angry soliloquy in waiting.

The Reader and the Writer

When I write, it is not with a pen
But with my blood—
My pain,
My wounds—
I spill the page red with everything that I know:
Everything that I was,
Everything that I am,
And everything that I will be.
The paper holds my past,
My present,
And my future.

People tell me they love my writing,
That my poetry is beautiful,
But that's so far from the truth.
There is no beauty in pain,
No blue skies on a rainy day.
I write because I am lost
As if the pen will take me home.
Deep down I know it never will,
Because home is where you are,
And where you are, I am not.

The Reader and the Writer

You were the one person I couldn't bring myself to write about.
I knew once your name touched the page, you'd live forever as I remembered you—
The one who made me feel every emotion all at once and so deeply,
The person who would be my someone,
The girl who made me want to do the things I'd never do.
Instead, you taught me how to do what I needed to do,
Like saying good-bye to you.
You showed me how to live without someone,
Someone I thought I'd never live without.
I'm worried that once I start writing,
I'd never want to stop.
I'd write about the beginning and the middle but never the end.
The end is still going on,
Like a dying, slow-burning flame.
I can't lie; I still wonder if you feel the same,
If you think there could be a sequel too—
A story that ends with me and you.

If poets had the talent of music,
We would sing at sold-out shows
Instead of giving our souls to silent little crowds.
We would hear them roar, women calling our names
Instead of getting semi-awkward stares and sad sullen eyes.
We would get to ride rowdy tour buses home,
But instead we often spend our nights alone.

The Reader and the Writer

When I lose myself in a good book, it almost reminds me of the depth of your eyes.

Those eyes of yours spoke more to me than thousands of words ever could.

They tell our story better than my poetry ever would:

Every emotion floating in your iris, the hue of love and hate;

The dilation signifying moments that frightened us and those that steadied us;

The sadness hides behind your pupils, leaving shadows of doubt every time you looked away.

All those years of pain had to be good for something—
Something to write about,
Something to look forward to.
It reminds me how much I love the taste of air,
How even when I feel like drowning, I am breathing.
And when the world stands still, my heart's still beating.
My veins may be filled with regret and longing,
But yet I am still here.
I am still alive.

The Reader and the Writer

The worst things that have happened to me have made me a better writer.
Without the heartache, disappointment, and sadness,
What could I possibly write about?
Happily ever after?
I stopped believing in those when I was eleven.

The more you don't love me,
The more I have to write.
Not out of self-pity,
Not out of spite,
But to remind myself I am still here…
Without you. Regardless of your existence.

The Reader and the Writer

You can probably tell by how I'm holding this pen
That I've been drinking again,
Thinking of the letters I'd never send,
Of you, and how we were back then;
Thinking of all the words never said
And all my messages left unread,
Hearing from them how great you've been,
Knowing I've played a game I'd never win.

The Drinker and the Drunk

The Drinker and the Drunk

Sitting at a table alone,
The glass is never empty.
The whiskey flows quickest
When my mind is racing the fastest,
When my heart is aching the hardest.

I could taste the cigarettes on your lips;
They tasted of slow death and shortened breaths.
I'm sure you could taste the whiskey on mine,
The quick burn and warmth that fades all too fast.

The Drinker and the Drunk

I've tried drinking to forget you.
I've swallowed shot after shot like it was my only cure.
I've forgotten my name, lost my wallet, and talked to
girls who looked like you.
I've blacked out and stumbled about.
I've gone home alone and some nights with them.
When she sheds her clothes, it may be her body,
But your name is all I can remember.

Written Words Never Spoken

When I am sober, I bottle it all inside.
When I have the bottle, it pours out—
Everything I never told you,
Everything I wish I told you.
The sting of whiskey hits the back of my throat
Like the sting of losing you.
I'll probably call you drunk.
I always do.
You never answer.

The Drinker and the Drunk

I couldn't resist. I called you again at 4:22 a.m. and told your voice mail all the things I could never say.
I wanted to tell you how I wished things were different, but they never are.
I'll tell your voice mail how long it took to work up the courage to call,
but part of me is glad you didn't answer. You didn't give me the chance to make myself a fool.
That's the beauty and tragedy of life: people will always come and go,
Some harder than others to let go.

I filled myself with smoke and drink,
Finding ways to dull the pain,
To make it all the more bearable.
But no matter how hard I inhale
And no matter how many bottles I empty,
It is always there, just below the surface,
Like a swimmer struggling to stay afloat.

The Sea and the Shore

The Sea and the Shore

The ship rocks back and forth.
I glance over the bow and see the storm.
With a turn of the wheel, I could be saved,
But I don't do a thing.
I sail toward the rain and thunder
And the perils of the sea.
Sometimes I think this is all because of me.
I don't deserve clear blue skies,
And I certainly didn't deserve you.
The ship has sailed off course for months;
I tossed the maps so long ago.
The hull groans and starts to splinter—
My hands bloodied and bones broken—
The salty blood mixes with the salty sea.
The ship is sinking, collapsing around me.

The hull was battered by the unrelenting waves.
Each crushing moment meant another loosened bolt and rusted panel.
The ship yearned for the coast, the safety in sandy beaches and coastal towns.
But you were my sea as well as my shore.

The Sea and the Shore

When the tides returned ashore, what was left of us came back with it—
Unrecognizable and waterlogged, faded with time—
Pieces of what we had would never be put back together no matter what we did or said.
All we could do was pass each other by like the lighthouse shining the way
To bring your ship home to another port,
A port that I wasn't at to welcome you home.

Our toes sat closely in the fine-grain sand.
Our hands interlaced as our eyes locked at sea.
Our hearts raced, and our stomachs fluttered;
The ocean mist filled the empty space.
In this moment, we were happy,
But like all moments, they pass with time.
Moments become memories and distant dreams—
They live on in faded photos,
In forgotten voice mails,
And in everything that reminds me of you.

The Sea and the Shore

The anchor dragged across the ocean floor,
Kicking up sand and shipwrecks of the past.
It brought to the surface everything
I've tried to forget.

They asked me how you are again, and I didn't know how to answer.
You weren't mine to watch over like a young child playing in the street,
And even if you were still the one I called my own, you didn't need that.
You were strong and smart and sometimes stubborn.
They ask as if you still call every afternoon and lie beside me every night.
Their faces twist and contort when I tell them that you're gone.
"Oh, you're better off without her" is all they can say,
Because deep down they know it's far from the truth.
You were the rope that tied my ship to shore and the light that guided me home if I started to drift.

The Sea and the Shore

In the middle of the ocean
Without land in sight,
Currents pulling
This way and that,
Unsure which way to swim,
So instead we choose to sink,
To drown in indecision—
When indecision becomes the decision,
When the world fades to black.

The Dark and the Light

The Dark and the Light

Your eyes as dark as the deepest sea
And you've caught the attention of only me.
I wonder why you sit there alone,
Singing along with only the saddest tone.
Your voice as calm as the darkest sky
And yet quiet I stay, passing you by,
Unknowing of what you were about to do…
If only I had taken the time to sit there with you.

Depression craves attention.
Like a needy child, it tugged on the bottom of my shirts
Until each and every one was threadbare and frayed.

The Dark and the Light

On a bathroom floor, she panicked and rang me twice.
She pretended not to know 911 and hoped I would be enough.
She hoped I cared enough to save her but not enough to stay.
With blood between the tiles, I tried, and I tried for a while.
The sobs turned to quiet breaths and comforting words,
But how do you convince someone to live when all he or she wants to do is die?

I tried to convince her that no matter how many times steel crossed flesh
And red spiraled down the bathroom sink, nothing would change.
The sky would still be blue and the grass still green,
And she still so very much wanted
That this life is as dark or as beautiful as you make it,
That the days can be filled with rain clouds and endless nights
or new beginnings and happy endings.
It will take time, no doubt, but she should know that I believe in her.

The Dark and the Light

Every battle I've fought, win or lose, I've walked alone.
It did not matter if I limped off the field or stood tall.
I only have myself to be proud of or to blame.
The victories and defeats rested beneath my feet or weighed on my shoulders alone.
I've crawled across finish lines, and sometimes I couldn't make it past the starter pistol.
Regardless the outcome, I always found a way to grow.

When there are days you feel like drowning,
Remember that you are made of water,
That even when you bear the weight of the world,
You will still float if you let yourself.
When every year has two winters, one a season and the other an emotion,
Remember that seasons change and so do feelings,
And every spring is a new chance at life.
It is time to let yourself grow and feel the sunlight.
When there are days that the sun cannot peek through the clouds,
Remember that there will always be a tomorrow,
And when the sun is high in a clear sky,
You will know that there is still a chance to live, to love, to forgive.
When you find that life gives you more questions than answers,
Remember that life is a one-way trip.
You may never get the answers you were looking for,
But that's not what's important—you are what's important.

The Knight and the Thief

The Knight and the Thief

I'd hold you if I could.
I'd save you if you'd let me
And sail away together at sea
To put the pieces back in place.
I'd be your hero and you, my heroine.
Our story would be center stage—
The spotlight on all the beautiful things.

If I could make it right, I would…
I would whisk away all the pain you've felt and feel,
But I am neither knight nor prince.
I am just a little boy who believed he could,
Who believed he would find his love and keep her close,
A boy who believed in her more than she did herself
To keep her safe from the monsters outside and in.

The Knight and the Thief

There were many dragons slain,
The curse of poisoned apples overcame,
Perilous seas sailed to find you—
All these feats done to prove myself worthy,
Worthy enough to be the one by your side.
Proud enough to call me your hero.
Unfortunately, though, this isn't a fairy tale.

I put so much time into helping others,
I didn't see what it was doing to me.
My hands were dry and calloused;
My voice cracked and coarse;
My legs heavy, bearing the burden of the world.
I gave everyone everything,
And there was nothing left for me.

The Knight and the Thief

All I wanted to do was save you,
Save you from monsters,
Save you from yourself,
But saving you took all the best parts of me,
And now that you're gone,
There's not much left for me.
I left a woman who taught me love
For one who showed me lust.
Now both are gone,
And I learned the word "alone."

I spent my life believing I'd find happiness in making someone else smile.
But the more I poured into others,
The more I hated myself in the mirror.
I gave away the best parts of me for people who only stayed until they were full.
When I was the one left empty and alone,
No one came back for me.

The Knight and the Thief

I questioned the words that escaped past my lips as much as the choices you made.
I know I wasn't perfect, and I know we would have our arguments.
But you were the one I wanted to have those with—
The woman I cared enough about to make you want to stay,
The one who could sway my heart like the limbs of trees in the autumn wind,
But all you did was strip the leaves, leaving me broken and bare.

The Seasons and the World

The Seasons and the World

The quiet stillness of a winter night brings me back.
It returns me to the days the sun just couldn't shine bright enough,
The memory of a time when no matter what I did, the snow kept falling,
Refusing to let me go outside even if just for fresh air.
I breathed in all the same pains and same desires.
I was a prisoner to a warm body in a cold world—sometimes I still am.
The baseboard heaters tried their best to bring warmth,
But I still fear one day there won't be any heat left,
And the world will come crashing in.

Spring was almost here,
And it was time I started cleaning,
Clearing the gutters of my heart,
Tossing my cupboards of you,
Throwing away faded frames,
Boxing up forgotten feelings.

The Seasons and the World

Winter was cold, brutal, and bleak.
In somber silence, alone I would weep.
Then we met in passing and didn't know
That together as people we would grow.
Spring was the start of something new,
Much like a morning's sun-kissed dew.
The feelings of love, we started to share.
To ruin something like this, we wouldn't dare.
Summer came; we laughed and loved,
With an endless blue sky floating above.
We would lie together, hand in hand.
The space between your fingers, mine would land.
Then autumn came, and leaves fell from the tree,
Left alone, standing there, only me.
That was our fall from grace…
Between my fingers, empty space.

On the first day of spring, it snowed.
Maybe to remind me that I—
Still had things to bury,
Feelings to push aside,
People to forget.
But the snow will eventually melt,
And everything once lost will be found again.

The Seasons and the World

In spring, everyone finds new blossoms.
They see the sun rise and set on vivid landscapes;
They take the chance to renew their lease on life,
But for me I'm left in winter.
I'm surrounded by the bitter cold and crippled trees.
I watch the endless nights blanket the earth.
I've spent so much time here, I'm less afraid of death
And more afraid of life.

Hidden underneath the steel beams and concrete structures,
We shy away from the nature that birthed us.
We have forgotten how the rain can sweep away the things we've tried to forget—
Things we tried to drown in liquor.
These monuments we construct get higher and bolder
While we shrink and falter.
They convince us that we are insignificant—
A speck of blood on an iron landscape.

The Seasons and the World

When I was in high school, I knew one too many girls who believed they weren't enough,
Consumed by thoughts their hands weren't big enough to hold.
So they stayed up too late and cussed too much.
When I was in college, I knew too many who held onto those thoughts.
Staying up too late became staying out till drunk.
And while they were stronger now, the world stayed cruel.
They were told to dream of a suburban home with a suburban man
But to also be free and travel and love freely and do this and do that,
And soon that teenage girl is just beneath the surface again,
Wondering how her hands or heart would ever be big enough.

We have outside pressures, telling us to live free,
That reason and responsibilities can wait,
To have fun and have many options,
To not act on one and lose all the others.
But in holding everything and everyone at arm's length,
And halfheartedly loving, we have made our choice—
The choice to find ourselves at thirty no better off than we were at twenty,
Except now those options are gone.
People have moved on.
Circumstances have changed.
The years spent endlessly searching, all for nothing.
We searched without a destination and fell in love with a journey we hoped would never end.

The Seasons and the World

The curse of the lost generation was akin to hopping bars.
Every bar meant a new drink, but each drink meant the same drunk.
The liquor sat heavy like the accumulation of condensation on crystal glass,
Every drop representing every moment that's happened thus far.
When glass meets tabletop, it falls to the bottom edge,
Forming a circular stain that would soak in if left too long.
Everything becomes muddled, mixing varied experiences into a singular result.
When this happens, it means it's time for the next bar,
Filled with the hope that this one would be the one.
There is an overwhelming disappointment when it's not.
So begins the jaded and callous continuation until last call.

Where the night sky met the rolling hills, we held each other—
The sound of our hearts louder than any words we could ever speak.
In our silence we relived and replayed every moment of good and bad,
Every moment that made us who we were, who we are, and who we will be.

The Stars and the Longing

The Stars and the Longing

I shout at the same night sky.
I reach for the same dying stars,
And the world still spins,
And I am still unheard.

Bearing the weight of the moon,
Its gravity pulled and tugged,
The oxygen slipped away,
And I with it.
I fell into the endless space,
Becoming black holes and stardust.

The Stars and the Longing

I was always constantly told my lack of worth.
I was told how incapable I was,
How insignificant I am.
But at the most basic level, I matter.
The little atoms inside were once a great star that lit up the night sky.
The flesh and bone that cover my soul can nurture trees and life when I'm gone.
So don't tell me I am worthless when every part of my being was once something great and will continue to be once I'm gone.

Without the busy city streets or billowed smoke stacks, the stars smiled down.
They bore every wish ever made and every dream that did or did not come true.
The stars wanted nothing more than to make skeptics believers and see the fruits of their labor.

The Stars and the Longing

I can't wait forever to be with you.
You have your life, and I have mine too.
I know we wish for you and I.
I dream, too, that our love never dies.
But sometimes there's nothing left to do
But to wonder my life without you.

Our lives consist of heartaches and endless strings of "almost,"
"Almost" being the most painful word—
The feeling of coming up short once again,
Being second place so many times—
Almost good enough.

The Stars and the Longing

I didn't know how to explain myself to you.
How somewhere between hello and today,
My feelings started to change.
I care about you the same but perhaps a little more.
I think you're just as gorgeous but perhaps a little more.
I don't think I can go back to how it was before,
Before your eyes spoke volumes to me
And before I started to wonder what we could be.

My words, if they come out at all, are jumbled and garbled in hesitant "I love yous."
When all I wanted to do was make you stay,
I feared by reaching out, I'd be pushing you away.
And maybe you'll never know how much I cared.
And I'll never have the chance to open the door or pull out a chair—
Kind gestures and words lost in translation,
Watching you watch someone else,
Letting feelings fade and desires diminish.

The Stars and the Longing

I didn't know what pain meant
Until I saw the way you looked at him
While I was looking at you.
You glanced over my shoulder
And spoke with so much desire and want,
More than I'd ever have the courage to say to you.

I have consistently considered the possibility of being alone,
Not by choice or by rejection
But by simply chance and circumstance—
The unlucky missed opportunities and the timing of it all.
There were moments here and there when I felt something more
That ran parallel to the times you were with someone who didn't know your favorite color.

The Stars and the Longing

A moment is all it would take,
But I'm worried that it won't matter what I say.
I'd spill my love in a mess of nervous words,
And you'd look at me the same
And kiss him like nothing's changed.

Whispers of the past and callings of the future petrified the present.
In reflecting on the past, time became wasted with what ifs.
In dreaming of the future, indecision plagued the now.
I knew how unhealthy this all was,
But the masochist in me enjoyed the longing and regret,
Reveled in the thoughts that morphed to letters so purposefully placed on paper,
Craved the power of loss more than possibility of happiness—
The intoxicating art of loss asphyxiated the reality of living.

The Stars and the Longing

Looking down into a cup of coffee,
I saw the universe floating in the steam.
I gazed upon all the endless possibilities.
I sat in awe and saw everything that has happened, is happening, and will happen.
In truth, looking into this cup and seeing the world was a lot like looking into your eyes,
Except in your eyes, I saw the endless ways to fall in love.

The Lover and the Dreamer

The Lover and the Dreamer

I can trace the veins on the back of your hand
Like streets and highways to your heart.
Each breath you take, fills your lungs
With blue skies and white clouds.
Your glance is warm as our earth's great sun,
And it always shines on me.

Burning logs of oak,
Warm crisp air,
Wind howling outside,
Wool blankets and white wine,
Whispered words of love,
Wrapped in each other's arms…
Wondering if this is it…
Is this as good as it gets?

Intimacy isn't when we're naked with the lights dimmed
With sweat on my brow and your breaths turned ragged.
Intimacy is when we speak with words all through the night,
With our hearts wide open just to see what's in our blood.

In my dreams, you came back to me.
It was the perfect scene—
In a small bar with dimly lit halls,
We danced all night.
Not a single care.
In a world of billions, just you and I…
You smiled, spun around in my arms,
And felt so safe;
I felt so needed.
Your back to my chest…
Your hair just under my nose…
You breathed so easy,
But your heart raced like mine.
I closed my eyes,
Hoping to stay forever.

The Lover and the Dreamer

I started to realize love wasn't about me or about you.
Love was about taking our perfectly flawed puzzle pieces
And creating something beautiful together—
Making the sum of our parts into a greater whole.
Working side by side for each other
Until a puzzle piece goes missing,
Swept beneath the rug or dropped behind the couch.

The Lost and the Found

The Lost and the Found

Every time I fell in love, it was never enough.
It happened so often that I have a box of leftover love sitting within my heart.
I keep telling myself that I'll just save it all for someone who's worth it,
That the next one is the one.
But I'm worried what happens when she opens that box.
What happens if all that love turned rotten and soured?
What happens if it comes out something else entirely?
What happens if it's a patchwork of past lovers that I'll try to make her out to be?
What happens if I really am just not enough?

I can throw rocks of blame around all night.
I can write passive-aggressive letters all day.
I can shout at the moon and the gods for cursing me,
But they are not the ones to blame.
I loaded my pockets with stones of regret and doubt.
I read between the lines and saw my own flaws.
I whispered to myself the truth I needed to hear.
After all was said and done, I was the one who was lost.

The Lost and the Found

If you listen closely to the pitter-patter of my heartbeat at night,
You'll hear it whisper your name,
Like it still feels safe there, close against my chest,
Like you're still bundled up under blankets and wrapped in my arms,
And sometimes if I wish hard enough and dream deep enough...
It's like you never left.
And other nights I awaken to the way you used to whisper my name.
How it sounded like forever right behind your teeth.
But it's all just a joke, and forever means until you've found someone better.

Written Words Never Spoken

I see and hear pieces of you in everything I do.
When I'm down by the shore, I watch the waves rush to the coast
Like how you used to run to me when you were scared or afraid,
But like the sea you'd soon retreat away and disappear.
When I listen to all my favorite songs, I remember yours.
You liked the same ones as I did, and I can hear you singing along.
You were always slightly off key, but that was just how I liked it.
When I'm at a red light, I am filled with ideas of hope.
I wanted so badly for you and I to be a we,
And yet the light turns green, and you're not sitting next to me.
When I close my eyes at night, you're all I see.
You're still in my arms, and we're still holding hands.
You look at me like I matter, like I mean something.
I see you right there against me, my legs tangled with yours.
I still feel the gentle ups and downs of your breathing.
I used to feel your warmth next to me, but now all I feel is cold.
When I pass a stranger and her eyes look like yours—
A lightish blue with a hint of green—
They catch my glance for only a second,
And for a second we fall in love,
The fleeting moment when everything is okay.
We believe that we can save each other,
But in truth we can't. Because she's not you. And you're already gone.

The Lost and the Found

I kept singing along to the same old song I thought you knew,
And I could have sworn, at times I heard you sing too.
But then I saw that you had turned the page.
Before you left you built me a mapless maze.
I stumbled around tripping over every word you said.
In the back of my mind, I knew I should have just fled.

I was always worried if I spoke the truth,
We would never speak again.
If I told you I loved you, it'd be the same as good-bye,
That if those words left my lips, it wouldn't be enough.
But the reality of the situation was far worse.
The words were just enough to make you stay.
We talk all the time,
But you don't love me too.
And I wish I could disappear from you.

The Lost and the Found

We danced ballet around those words.
You knew where our lives were headed toward—
Step left; step right, our love misaligned.
If and only if we had more time.
The chorus came; I pulled you near.
The bridge beckoned; I said what you feared.
You fell back; I knew I lost you.
You can't bring yourself to say "I love you too."

Written Words Never Spoken

What I expected was a little decency,
That you'd have the heart to tell him what you did.
To tell him what you do when he doesn't answer you,
To speak the truth even you don't want to hear.
How can you look at me the way you do
when you lie with him at night?
How could you do that to me?
How can you lay with me at night
when you look at him the way you do?
How could you do that to him?

The Lost and the Found

In my nightmares, he and I trade places.
I become the boyfriend
And he the lover
He becomes the cause of my insecurity,
And I become his green jealousy

Graduation is a time for good-byes—
A good-bye to friends,
A good-bye to places,
Good-bye to a great time.
It marks the start of something new,
When everything after is a little bleaker.
Graduation means growing up,
And growing up means growing old.

The Lost and the Found

Win some, lose some.
Lose some more
Until there's nothing left to lose.
How freeing it must be.

I know pain like he's my older brother
And know joy like she's my little sister.
I am the middle child stuck between the two.

The Lost and the Found

Years have passed, and I still remember you.
I remember your voice.
I remember your smile.
I remember your heartbeats.
I most certainly remember your love,
And every day I feel its absence.

The photos I've taken are more beautiful than the people I've loved.
I wrapped the walls with pictures of the places I've been to.
I thought if I didn't, I would forget them like you forgot me.

The Lost and the Found

People say the best things in life are free,
But so are the worst.
A night alone.
An empty bed.
An empty home.
An empty life.
A lost love.
A dying friend.
All for free.

At the crossroads of nostalgia and regret,
I wanted to remember, but I wanted to forget.
I found myself between letting go and holding on.

The Lost and the Found

Now that I have been alone for X amount of time,
I saw the many variables that kept me from being happy—
Every force, outside and in, working against me in every way,
And though it's selfish to say the world is out to get me,
It certainly feels that way now and again.

The long good-bye would recount every moment we've shared
Like the times we've taken drives to a moonlit beach
Or whenever we'd just go to get groceries.
The long good-bye would retrace everything I've said to show you I care
Like how I would always tell you to text me when you got home,
How I'd tell you to put on your seat belt even before the car tells you to.
The short good-bye would simply be "I loved you once."

The Lost and the Found

Months after you've been gone,
You're still the best thing that's ever happened to me.
I began to be who I ought to be and ground my dreams in reality.
I worked tirelessly, almost as relentlessly as I tried to keep you close to me.
You showed me that sometimes things just cannot be and how nothing is what it seems.
You taught me to focus on what is in my hands and what I can do
And learn to let everything else slip through,
But sometimes when my mind drifts, it's the thoughts of you it'll find.
If your absence helped me achieve so much, I start to wonder what we could have done together.

Even though I know how horrible it is,
Sometimes I wish you would have died—
Died in a car accident,
Whisked away by a deadly disease—
Because then I would only lose you once.
I would mourn your death
and remember the times we loved.
Instead I lose you all the time, every day.
I lose you when you lose yourself in his eyes.
I wish I was still who you wanted.
I lose you when I talk to another girl.
She never says things the way you did.
I lose you when I see you smile and I'm not the reason.
I miss the way your lips curl before you burst into laughter.
I lose you every day that you are alive.
I've lost myself because you made me feel alive.

The Lost and the Found

When she told me she'd never want me,
What she really meant was she never wanted what I wanted.
She wanted to stay but not in my arms or with hands locked with mine.
She wanted me to miss her when she wasn't there
But never wanted me to kiss her.
She said she wanted us to stay friends,
But how could we ever be friends when I never saw her as a friend?
There is nothing wrong with what she wanted.
There's nothing wrong with what I thought I needed.
We were just two people with wishful thinking.
She wanted less, and I wanted more.

We reached an understanding that we would never have each other.
But that didn't stop us from dreaming.
She dreamed of her back pressed to my chest in the kitchen,
Of quiet nights with just each other's presence.
I wished we could lie in the grass and wish upon the stars.
But dreams were just as far away
Passing us by like highway-speed cars.
You'd be traveling east, and I'd be going west,
But together this dream was headed south.

The Lost and the Found

I was caught up on small words and past actions…
So consumed by little nothings that piled up to something more.
The words loomed over me like clouds full of rain,
And the actions were cement shoes that drowned me in the puddle of words.
I could not escape even if I tried.
I shoulder the weight still to this day.
Whether or not it's made me stronger
Is yet to be seen.

Just once, I would like "I love you" full stop.
Not "I love but…"
Or "I'd love you if…"
Simply "I love you"—
A love that didn't need reason or rhythm,
A love that was reason enough,
and a love that beat to its own drum.

The Lost and the Found

Even after changing bedsheets and scrubbing floors,
I can still smell the lingering scent of your shampoo,
And I still find your clothes at the bottom of laundry bins,
No matter how many times I do the wash.
You are always with me, like a looming shadow—
A constant reminder of what I have lost.

A box of bad memories.
A blue hair tie on the floor.
Bobby pins in the bathroom.
Your forgotten shirt between my bed and nightstand.
Your toothbrush right next to mine.
All these things meant so little at the time,
But now they sit in a box of memories
I only dare open on your birthday and our would-be anniversary.

www.ingramcontent.com/pod-product-compliance
Lightning Source LLC
Chambersburg PA
CBHW031449040426
42444CB00007B/1036